# Table of Cont

Essential Question

# Where do ideas for inventions come from?

# Solving Problems
# Through
# Technology

## Solving Problems Through Technology

### Student Objectives
*I will be able to:*

- Read and analyze informational texts about inventions and inventors.

- Share ideas with my peers.

- Build my vocabulary knowledge.

- Write informational, narrative, and opinion texts.

Credits
Editor: Cindy Peattie
Creative Director: Laurie Berger
Art Directors: Melody DeJesus, Kathryn DelVecchio-Kempa, Doug McGredy, Chris Moroch
Production: Kosta Triantafillis
Director of Photography: Doug Schneider
Photo Assistant: Jackie Friedman

Photo credits: Table of Contents A, Page 5, 14C, 15B, 16, 17A, 18, 19A, 20, 21A, 21G, 21I: The Granger Collection, NYC; Table of Contents B, Page 12C: © H. Mark Weidman Photography/Alamy; Page 6: ClassicStock.com/Superstock; Page 7C: © Wolff & Tritschler/Corbis; Page 8C: NaturePL/Superstock; Page 8D: © Scott Camazine/Alamy; Page 9A, 26, 27, 28, 29A, 29B, 30, 32A: AP Images; Page 12B: © Frank Conlon/Star Ledger/Corbis; Page 13: Courtesy of Lacy Snarr; Page 14A: © CORBIS; Page 14B, 14D, 19B: Library of Congress; Page 21F: © Underwood & Underwood/Corbis; Page 21H: © Scott Camazine/Alamy; Page 24: © Oleksiy Maksymenko Photography/Alamy; Page 31: AMELIE-BENOIST/BSIP/Newscom; Page 33: NASA

Illustrations: Monica Armino p.25

Permissions: "Crazy Boys" from *Hand in Hand: An American History Through Poetry*, copyright 1994 by Beverly McLoughland. Reprinted by permission of Beverly McLoughland.

Printed in Dongguan, China. 8557/1218/15247

ISBN: 978-1-4900-9185-3

# Tips for Text Annotation

**As you read closely for different purposes, remember to annotate the text. Use the symbols below to annotate.**

| Symbol | Purpose |
|---|---|
| underline | Identify a key detail. |
| ☆ | Star an important idea in the margin. |
| ① ② ③ | Record a sequence of events. |
| (jealous) | Circle a key word or phrase. |
| ? | Mark a place in the text where you have a question. Write your question in the margin. |
| ! | Mark a place in the text where you have an idea. Write your idea or thought in the margin. |

### Your annotations might look like this.

> Notes
>
> 1  Many moons ago, there lived a (brave) ① warrior. He was called the Invisible One. ☆ No one could see him except his sister. He pledged to marry the first woman who could see him.
>
> *What does the word callous mean?*
>
> *I wonder why she was called Rough-Face Girl.*
>
> 2  Nearby, there lived a man with two daughters. The elder daughter was callous ? and cruel. The younger, called Rough-Face ! Girl, was gentle and kind. Rough-Face Girl worked hard. She tended the fire. It made her face rough and chapped. Her idle sister did nothing. ②
>
> 3  One day, Idle Sister announced, "I want to marry the Invisible One!" She hurried ③

LEXILE® is a trademark of MetaMetrics, Inc., and is registered in the United States and abroad.

E-book and digital teacher's guide available at benchmarkuniverse.com.

**BENCHMARK EDUCATION COMPANY**
145 Huguenot Street • New Rochelle, NY • 10801

**Toll-Free 1-877-236-2465**
**www.benchmarkeducation.com**
**www.benchmarkuniverse.com**

**Shared Reads 1 & 2**

Remember to annotate as you read.

Notes

# Anna Connelly: Inventor

1    Over 100 years ago, fire was a danger for people in city apartment buildings. When fire swept through a building, people on the upper floors were trapped.

2    In 1887, Anna Connelly designed a steel staircase. The staircase attached to the outside of buildings. Now, people had a way to get out of burning buildings. Anna's fire escape saved many lives all over the country.

# Crazy Boys

by Beverly McLoughland

Watching buzzards,
Flying kites,
Lazy, crazy boys
The Wrights. They
Tried to fly
Just like a bird
Foolish dreamers
Strange. Absurd. We
Scoffed and scorned
Their dreams of flight.
But we were wrong
And they were Wright.

Remember to annotate as you read.

Notes

# A Woman with Vision

1    Would you ride in a car if the driver were wearing a blindfold? No way! Yet years ago, drivers had no way to see through their windshield when snow and rain obscured their vision. Drivers had to stop and get out. They had to clear a spot on the windshield to see through and then drive on.

▲ Years ago, a driver had to clear the windshield by hand.

2     In 1903, Mary Anderson was riding in a streetcar in unpleasant weather. She noticed drivers constantly stopping to scrape and rescrape their windshields. She thought there had to be a better way. She invented a window-clearing device that drivers controlled from inside their cars. Those first wipers were manual, not motorized. But they changed cars and driving forever.

▲ Anderson was in a streetcar like this one when she got the idea that changed driving forever.

Notes

# A Lucky Accident

1    Some scientists work for years hoping to invent something but never doing so. Others invent things when they're not even trying. George de Mestral found his invention by accident. After walking outdoors, George's overcoat and his dog's fur were covered in prickly plants called burrs. George wondered what made their grip so strong.  He looked closely. He noticed tiny hooks on the burrs.

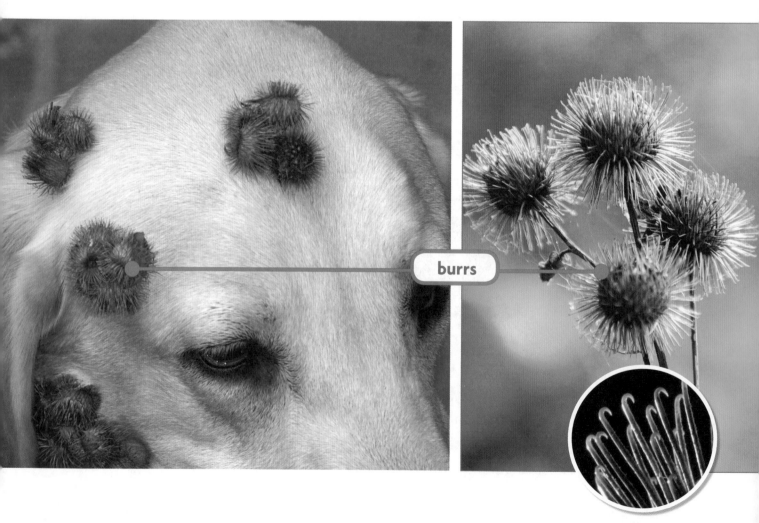

burrs

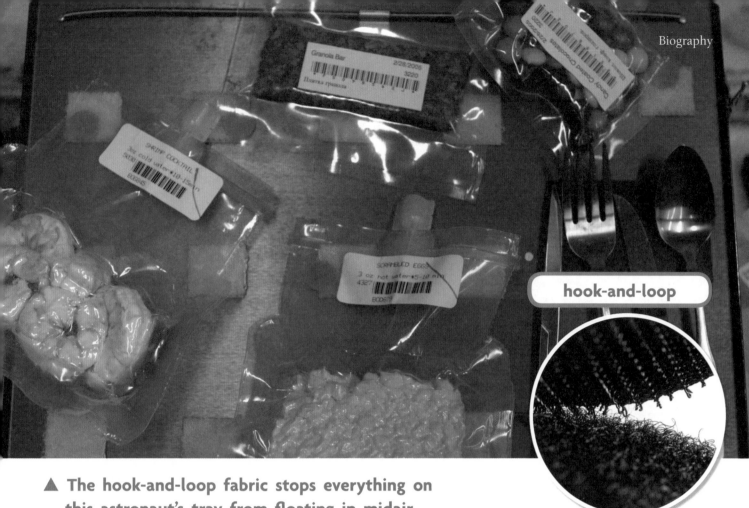

hook-and-loop

▲ The hook-and-loop fabric stops everything on this astronaut's tray from floating in midair.

2    George found that those hooks caught on anything with loops, such as fabric, or cloth, and fur. That hook-and-loop discovery became famous. Zippers, shoelaces, and snaps can be hard for the very young and people with disabilities to use. But almost everyone can press and pull this sticky fabric. Astronauts even use it to hold down stuff in space!

Notes

# Kid Inventors

1    Who invented the TV? Who made the first earmuffs? Whose mistake led to the yummy ice pop? The answer to all these questions is . . . a kid! Boys and girls have always been able to invent many useful things. Some of these inventions might even amaze you!

2    Hart Main is a kid inventor. He didn't like his sister's candles. They smelled like things only girls would like. So he said, "I'll invent candles for boys!" He got wax and stuff to make different scents, or smells. Then he got old soup cans. He made candles that smelled like coffee, bacon, baseball mitts, and freshly cut grass. They were a big hit!

3    Ben Franklin was an inventor long ago. He started inventing things when he was a little kid, too. January 17 is his birthday. Now it's Kid Inventor Day, a day to celebrate kids' great ideas. On this day, you could start a kid inventors' club and invite your friends. Or, jot down invention ideas in a notebook and make something. No matter how simple, your invention could dazzle the world!

# BuildReflectWrite

## Build Knowledge

Describe the inventions in "A Woman with Vision" and "A Lucky Accident." Explain how these inventions helped people solve problems.

| Invention | Problem | Solution |
|---|---|---|
|  |  |  |
|  |  |  |

## Reflect

**Where do ideas for inventions come from?**

Based on this week's texts, write new ideas and questions you have about the essential question.

_____

_____

_____

_____

_____

_____

## Write to Sources

**Narrative**

After reading "A Woman with Vision" and "A Lucky Accident," imagine you invented something that helped you solve a problem. Write a short story describing your invention. Your narrative should use facts and details you have learned from the reading selections.

Remember to annotate as you read.

Notes

# A Colorful Invention

1    The next time you open a box of crayons, you can thank two cousins for their colorful invention.

2    Edwin Binney and Harold Smith made pencils and chalk. They sold these items to schools. They wanted colorful, safe, and affordable drawing tools for children. They used wax and pigments to create crayons.

3    The first boxes of crayons had eight colors. They were sold in 1903. Crayons are just as popular today!

# Eletelephony

by Laura E. Richards

Once there was an elephant,
Who tried to use the telephant—
No! No! I mean an elephone
Who tried to use the telephone—

(Dear me! I am not certain quite
That even now I've got it right.)

Howe'er it was, he got his trunk
Entangled in the telephunk;
The more he tried to get it free,
The louder buzzed the telephee—
(I fear I'd better drop the song
Of elephop and telephong!)

Notes

# Famous Inventors

by Margaret McNamara

## Introduction

1    An inventor is someone who creates something new. An inventor also finds new ways to do things. An inventor works to solve problems.

2    Get ready to meet and read about three famous inventors. They were also scientists. Find out what they invented. Learn what problems they solved. See how their inventions changed the way people live every day.

**Thomas Alva Edison**          **Alexander Graham Bell**          **George Washington Carver**

# Thomas Alva Edison (1847–1931)

3     Thomas Alva Edison loved to read and to learn. He also loved to try to make new things. In 1869, he came up with his first big invention. He made improvements to a machine used by the stock market. His invention was so good that he was paid $40,000. That is like one million dollars today. Edison decided to become a full-time inventor. That turned out to be good for the entire world.

▼ On August 12, 1877, Edison invented the first phonograph.

4    During his lifetime, Edison and his workers came up with more than 1,000 inventions. He is best known for inventing the first long-lasting electric lightbulb. He also invented the phonograph. The first phonograph made recordings of people talking or singing. He invented the first movie camera, too. When you are up one night watching a movie or listening to music, think about Thomas Edison.

▲ Edison tested the first successful incandescent lamp.

# Alexander Graham Bell (1847–1922)

5     Alexander Graham Bell had a lifelong interest in communication. He was also interested in the human voice. Bell's mother was deaf. His father was a speech teacher. In 1872, Bell began to tutor deaf children. He also worked to make a better telegraph. A telegraph sends and receives coded sound messages. The sounds were beeps and clicks. Each sound stood for a letter. A telegraph was the only way people could "talk" to each other from far away.

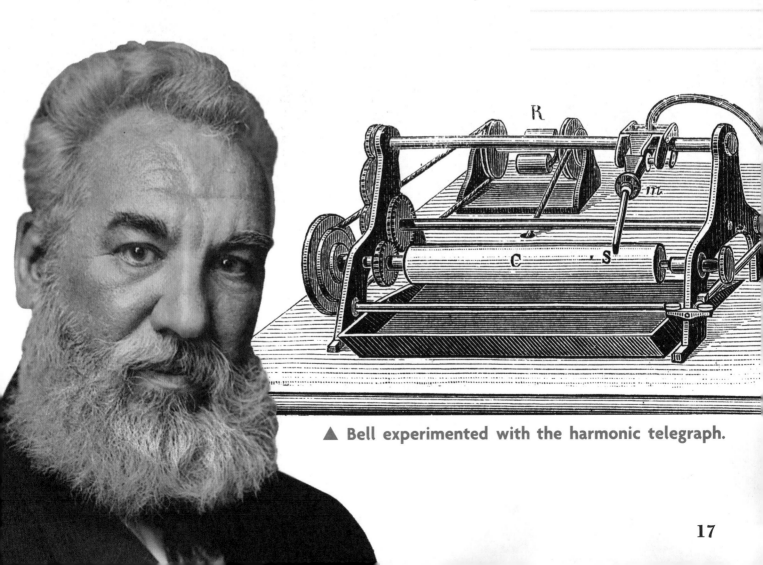

▲ **Bell experimented with the harmonic telegraph.**

6     Bell wanted to invent a machine that would send and receive the human voice. He worked on his idea for years. In 1876, Bell showed the world the first telephone. People in different places could now hear one another's voices!

# George Washington Carver (1864–1943)

7    George Washington Carver was an African American. He was born a slave in Missouri. Slavery ended in 1865. As Carver grew up, he loved to learn about plants. When he was old enough, Carver went to college. He was the first black student at Iowa State Agricultural College. He studied everything he could about plants.

▲ Southern farmers grew only cotton.

8    After college, Carver became a teacher. He taught students and farmers about plants. Most farmers in the southern United States grew cotton. Carver wanted them to grow other plants as well. He knew that would help farmers make more money. He knew it would be good for the soil, too.

9    Carver taught farmers how to grow peanut plants. He taught them how to grow sweet potato plants, too. He invented hundreds of new uses for peanuts and sweet potatoes. Because of Carver, farmers had better lives. And everyone benefited from his inventions.

▲ Carver invented ways to make ink, soap, and glue from peanuts.

## Inventors

| Thomas Edison | Alexander Graham Bell | George Washington Carver |

## Inventions

phonograph

lightbulb

telephone

peanuts

ink

soap

sweet potatoes

## Conclusion

10    Inventors create new things. They also work to solve problems. Some inventors make things that change the way people live.

11    Other inventors find better ways to do things. The inventors in this book all changed the world for the better.

# The Curious Boy

1    Tom Edison was a curious boy. He was always asking questions like *Why?* and *How?* When he couldn't get answers, he did experiments. Finding the answers to his questions brought him great joy.

2    When Tom was a boy, he didn't have a lot of toys. So one day he went to the barn to play. He spotted some geese that weren't making any noise. They were just sitting on their eggs to hatch them. Tom wanted to know what would happen if he sat on eggs. Would they hatch, too? So Tom placed a few eggs in a nest and sat down. What happened? *Splat!*

3    Tom also spotted birds eating worms. He knew birds could fly. He wondered if people ate worms, could they fly, too? So, Tom chopped up some worms and put them into a glass of water. He asked a girl to drink it. What happened? She got sick. And no, she didn't fly.

4    Tom went on to do many more experiments. He would turn some of them into inventions that still help families today. Tom would grow up to join the list of the greatest inventors of all time!

# BuildReflectWrite

## Build Knowledge

Based on your reading of "Famous Inventors," identify the inventions and their impact on society.

| Inventors | Inventions | Impact |
|---|---|---|
| Thomas Alva Edison | | |
| Alexander Graham Bell | | |
| George Washington Carver | | |

## Reflect

### Where do ideas for inventions come from?

Based on this week's texts, write new ideas and questions you have about the essential question.

_____

_____

_____

_____

_____

_____

## Write to Sources

### Informative/Explanatory

Drawing on "Famous Inventors" and "A Woman with Vision," write a short essay that explains what led to the inventions of the telephone and windshield wipers. In your essay, describe how these inventions affected people's lives. Use facts and details from the two reading selections as the basis of your explanation.

# A Robot That Cleans

by Kathy Kafer

1   Do you wish you had a robot to clean your room? Two students wanted to find out how to help people do chores.

2   Helen Greiner and Colin Angle were interested in robots. They wanted to find ways to use robots in homes. Together, they invented a small robot. It rolls over floors vacuuming dust, crumbs, and dirt. Maybe their next idea will be a robot that can put toys away!

# A Smart Pillow

1    Lin had a big spelling test the next day. She had studied for hours. Now, as her head hit the pillow, she wished there were an easier way to learn how to spell.

2    That night, Lin dreamed she invented a pillow that connected to a special port in her spelling book. Then, while she slept, the words were uploaded into her brain!

3    When Lin awoke, she found the book under her pillow. In school that day, she aced the test. But Lin knew it wasn't the pillow that was smart!

Remember to annotate as you read.

Notes

# Robots Go to School

by Kathy Kafer

1    It's a school morning. Drew wakes up and gets dressed. He eats breakfast. But instead of getting on the school bus, he turns on his computer. Drew stays home and sends his robot to school.

2    This isn't a day in the future. It's not a scene from a movie. For Drew, it's just a regular school day.

3    Special robots now go to school for some children. They help children like Drew who cannot be in a classroom. Most of these children are too sick to go to school. They have to stay home. Some are in the hospital. These children can get sick from being around other kids. School is dangerous for them.

4    Teachers could go to these children and give them lessons. But teachers cannot keep these children from getting lonely. They want to be with other kids. They miss their friends. They miss being a part of school activities. These special robots let children who can't go to school feel as if they are there.

## How School Robots Work

5    Some students use robots when they have to stay in a hospital for a long time. On his computer screen, Nate sees everything the school robot sees. If the teacher does a math problem, Nate watches her. Nate hears the teacher talk. He can also hear what the other students say. From the hospital, Nate can ask questions. He can talk to his friends.

6    The robot has a video screen. Nate's face shows up on that screen. If he wants to answer a question, he presses a button. A light flashes on the robot. The teacher knows to call on Nate.

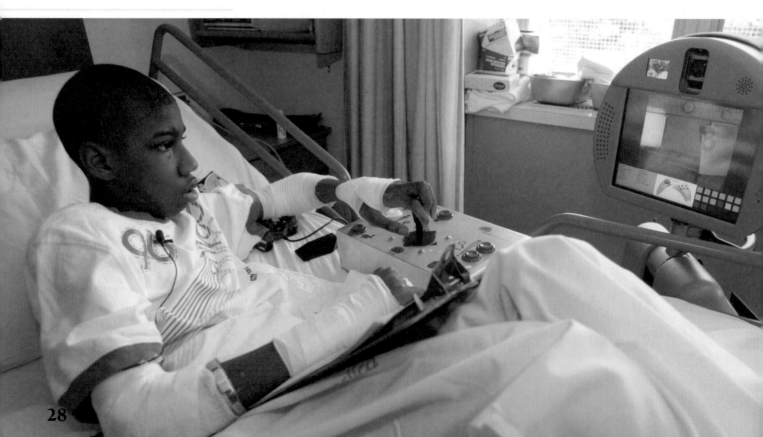

7    The robot has wheels. It can move around a classroom. It can travel up and down the hallways. It can go to art or music class. The robot can even line up with the other children during a fire drill.

8    How does the robot move? Nate moves the robot with his computer mouse. A signal is sent through the Internet to the robot. And the robot sends videos back to Nate.

## In the Classroom

9    The children who use school robots often give them nicknames. Some nicknames are "Princess Robot" and "Rob Robot Boy." Some children dress up their robots. The robot might wear the child's favorite T-shirt or bright ribbons. On the child's birthday, the robot goes to school with a crown.

10    The other children think school robots are special, too. They often forget that the robot is a robot. Instead, they just see their friend. They talk to their friend just as if he or she is there with them. They call out to the robot in the hallway and say good-bye when they go home.

▲ A school robot leads the line.

▲ A school robot helps a teacher.

11    Teachers like having these robots, too. The robots let teachers keep in touch with their sick students. Teachers can even give classroom jobs to children at home. Drew's robot, for example, is the classroom "greeter."

12    Of course, school robots are not real children. They cannot think or talk on their own. They don't learn for the children who use them. Those children still have to pay attention. They still have to turn in homework and get assignments signed.

13  Also, the robots look nothing like real children. They have no arms or legs. Their bodies are short and rounded. Their "heads" are video screens. And instead of feet, they have wheels.

14  The robots have limitations. They cannot climb stairs or open doors. Sometimes they bump into things. When the Internet is down, the sick child cannot tell the robot what to do. The robot stops moving and talking. The child can no longer see what is going on at school.

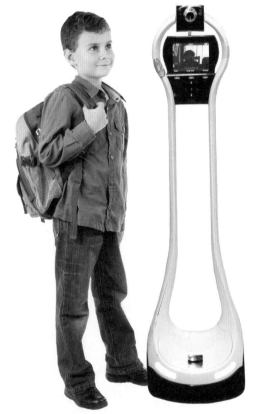

## The Future of School Robots

15    People are finding new ways to use school robots. Some robots help teach children with special needs. In South Korea there are not many English teachers. The real teachers live far away. So the English teachers send robots to the schools.

16    A school robot comes with a high price: $6,000. People are working to lower the cost. They are also making these special robots better. They will be easier to use. They will climb stairs and open doors and do much more. The future may be closer than you think!

## Robots in the Real World

Our world is filled with robots. Some robots are smaller than school robots. Others are much bigger. Many robots work in factories. They make cars, cell phones, and even candy bars. Other robots work in hospitals. They help doctors treat sick people. Robots do dangerous jobs. They get rid of bombs. They go places people cannot go, such as the ocean floor. Robots help explore outer space.

# Robots

1     There are many kinds of robots. There are robots that can clean. There are robots that can go. There are even robots that can read, write, and count. Wow!

2     Robots come in many shapes and sizes. Some robots are big and look like us. They have arms, legs, and a head. Other robots are small. They are round like a ball or flat like a plate. Do you wonder what the next robots might look like? Scientists are looking at animals for ideas. One robot they're making looks like an elephant's snout, or nose. It will be used like an arm. It will help people move or pick up things.

3     Another robot looks like a small bird. It doesn't make a sound. It will be used to see what's happening down on the ground. There's also a robot that looks like a bee. It buzzes around flowers but doesn't sting. It will be used to help crops grow.

4     What kind of robot would you want? What if scientists made a robot that could help you with your homework? Now what would you think about that?

# BuildReflectWrite

## Build Knowledge

Think about children like Drew who cannot be in the classroom. What are some ways special robots help sick children stay connected at school? List your ideas in the space provided.

| How Special Robots Help Sick Children |
|---|
|  |

## Reflect

**Where do ideas for inventions come from?**

Based on this week's texts, write new ideas and questions you have about the essential question.

_____

_____

_____

_____

_____

_____

## Write to Sources

**Opinion**

Of all the inventions you read about in this unit, which do you think has been the most helpful to people's lives? Why? In a short essay, state your opinion and provide reasons to support it. Use evidence from two of the reading selections to support your opinion and reasons.

# Support for Collaborative Conversation

## Discussion Prompts

**Share a new idea or opinion . . .**

I think that _____.

I notice that _____.

My opinion is _____.

An important event was when _____.

**Gain the floor . . .**

I would like to add _____.

Excuse me for interrupting, but _____.

That made me think of _____.

**Build on a peer's idea or opinion . . .**

I also think that _____.

In addition, _____.

Another idea is _____.

**Express agreement with a peer's idea . . .**

I agree with [Name] because _____.

I agree that _____.

I think that is important because _____.

**Respectfully express disagreement . . .**

I disagree with [Name] because _____.

I understand your point of view, but I think _____.

Have you considered that _____?

**Ask a clarifying question . . .**

What did you mean when you said _____?

Are you saying that _____?

Can you explain what you mean by _____?

**Clarify for others . . .**

I meant that _____.

I am trying to say that _____.

## Group Roles

**Discussion Facilitator:**
Your role is to guide the group discussion and make sure that everyone has the chance to participate.

**Scribe:**
Your job is to record the ideas and comments your group members share.

**Timekeeper:**
You will keep track of how much time has passed and help keep the discussion moving along.

**Encourager:**
Your role is to motivate and support your group members.

36